The referee blew.

Lucas counted one . . . two . . . thr

Then everything went quiet.

He closed his eyes. Opened them.

Then he struck the ball.

3

As soon as the ball hit the back of the net, Lucas was
mobbed by his team mates.

He smiled. They'd won. They were through to the
next round of the cup.

And Lucas had that brilliant feeling inside.
The feeling of scoring a goal.

Everyone had known that Lucas would score.
Because Lucas was the best in the world at one thing.

Better than Messi.

Better than Ronaldo.

Better than Rooney.

Lucas Wetherall took penalties. And he *never* missed.
Ever.

But all that was about
to change. The next
Saturday, Lucas's team were
playing in a league game.
They were already
winning 3-0. Then their
striker was brought down.

The referee blew his whistle.

Penalty!

As always, Lucas placed
the ball on the spot.

As always, he counted
to three.

As always, he closed and
opened his eyes.

Then Lucas stepped up.
Struck the ball.

And missed.

That night Lucas couldn't sleep. He was gutted that he'd missed the penalty.

He couldn't remember ever feeling so down.

He listened to the soft voices of his mum and dad through his bedroom wall.

But it didn't help.

He wanted to pretend that everything was normal.

After all, the football had been OK. Although Lucas had missed the penalty, his team had still won. None of his team mates blamed him for missing.

But everything else wasn't normal.

Not anymore.

He was afraid.

What if he never scored a penalty again?

After a week of worry, Saturday finally arrived.

Lucas's dad knocked on his bedroom door to wake him.

"I'm not getting up," Lucas said.

"What?" Dad asked, putting his head round the door.

"I don't feel so good," Lucas fibbed.

"Lucas, you can't let the team down," Dad argued.

"Tell them I'm injured," Lucas replied.

"Don't be silly," Dad said. He pulled the Leeds United duvet off Lucas's bed. "Come on."

"This is about the penalty, isn't it?" Lucas's dad said as he drove to the football club.

Lucas shrugged.

Dad pressed on. "Look. Everyone misses penalties."

"I don't," Lucas snapped.

They turned into the football club car park.
Lucas felt hot and his throat was dry. Should he
tell his dad the truth?

"I'm scared," Lucas mumbled. "I'm scared we'll get
a penalty today and . . ."

". . . and you'll miss?" Dad finished his sentence.

"Do you like scoring goals?" Dad asked Lucas.

"Yes," Lucas said, thinking back to how it felt.

Dad showed Lucas a white scar running down his leg.

"When I was your age, I fell off my bike. Badly. I never rode a bike again."

"You did," Lucas said. "You ride with me all the time."

"True," Dad said. "But I didn't ride my bike again for a long, long time. I only started again so I could ride with you."

"So?" Lucas asked.

"So, don't do what I did. Don't give in to your fear. Don't waste years not doing something you love."

14

15

Just after half time, Lucas's team was awarded a penalty.

As always, the ball was tossed to Lucas.

He tried to ignore his fear. His arms felt tingly.

His face was hot.

He knew the eyes of 50 people – at least – were
on him. Expecting him to score.

Lucas spotted the ball and breathed in deeply.

He stepped back and looked around him.
He saw the smiles and nods from his team mates.
They all thought he would score.
None of them had any doubts at all.

But Lucas did.

Lucas saw his dad on the far side of the pitch.
Thumbs up and smiling.

He swallowed.

Then he counted one . . . two . . . three . . .

Lucas closed his eyes. He remembered what his dad had said.

Don't do what I did. Don't waste years not doing something you love.

No, Lucas said to himself, I'm not going to do that.

Lucas opened his eyes, stepped up to the ball and struck it.

Lucas's feelings

happy

shocked

worried

confident

nervous

grumpy

23

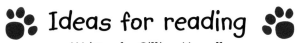

Ideas for reading

Written by Gillian Howell
Primary Literacy Consultant

Learning objectives: *(reading objectives correspond with Purple band; all other objectives correspond with Ruby band)* read independently and with increasing fluency longer and less familiar texts; know how to tackle unfamiliar words that are not completely decodable; deduce characters' reasons for behaviour from their actions; create roles showing how behaviour can be interpreted from different viewpoints

Curriculum links: Citizenship, P.E.

Interest words: referee, whistle, penalty, quiet, goal, league, argued, injured, ignore, tingly, doubts

Resources: pens, paper

Word count: 744

Getting started

- Read the title with the children and discuss the cover illustration. Ask the children to explain what they know about football and how penalties play a part in the game. Ask them if they think this book will tell a story or give them information and why they think that.

- Turn to the back cover and read the blurb together to confirm the children's ideas about the type of book this is.

Reading and responding

- Ask the children to read up to the end of p14 quietly. Listen in and prompt as necessary.

- Remind the children to use their knowledge of phonics and contextual clues to help them work out words they are unsure about. Point out the word *whistle* on p2 and ask them to think of other words they know that begin with *wh*, e.g. *who* or *what*. Point out that the *t* is silent.